POEMS I SHOULDN'T WRITE

Poems I Shouldn't Write

SOJOURNER DAVIDSON

LCCN: 2025922877

First Edition

Tending Verses, LLC

Fairfax, VA

tendingverses.com

CW: Abuse, Depression, Violent Imagery, Body Horror, Internalized Ableism

To every ace and enby
To all those who are still waiting to be chosen
Always choose yourself first
To those who have been told you're too much
Love with your open heart
<3 <3 <3

The Undercover House

After Robert Frost

I'll write about the road
Less traveled
And the house that stands empty
I'll write about the frigid
Puffs of wind
To my face
As I walk on this lonely road
I will stop to stare at the empty
House
I will wonder
What ghosts
Would befriend me
If I were to enter
I will remember ghosts are hungry
For the living
I will come across the empty house
On the path
Only I can see
I will come across the empty house
And wonder
Did I not just pass
This
Some tether will pull on me
And I will walk across the icy snow
To the tooth white door
It will swing on its hinges
Like it's been expecting me
I will enter a house
Not so empty
Almost bursting
With colorfully dressed beings

7

Dancing and Sitting
Eating and Reading
Talking and Listening
I will look over my shoulder
And see
Many more paths
Converge
On what has always looked
So empty

Poems I Shouldn't Write

The love poem
The confessional
The sad enby poem

I'm sure I've left out
A few

Here, a sad enby confessional:

I used to think
I could love you

Someday
Maybe I will

Someday

But not
With the same desire
I once had

Desire and love
They aren't the same

Desire drives a hole
In me

Makes a wild alter
To the empty

Does this make you sad

Did I confess enough

Do you know I don't
Believe anyone will love
Me in the way I love them

Do you know I am afraid
To show anyone my bareness

No, I want to show you all
That is inside

I am talking about the skin
I am talking about the chest
I am afraid somebody
Will marvel
At my flesh

Forget to see me
As who I am

Is this confession enough

Do you want more of me

Too bad

This is all I have
For
Now

This is all I have for you

Mirror of Your Beauty

Saw lilies in your hair
One day
Wanted
To pick them out
And give them
Back to you
Once painted
Into your portrait
You frown
And smile
The way you do
My lips make the same
Shape on accident
Carried a bit away
A bit too far

You Are a House with Many Doors

Your heart is at its center
And all the doors open
To that dripping red muscle
People wander in
Learn to hear a different rhythm
While making their own
Beats work together
You rarely close your doors

Bust(ed)

Try to love me
My droughty
Skin
Cracked and frosty
Lips
Bruised, scarred, stretch
Marked
Skin
Tongue with fat taste buds
Gapped teeth
Unsymmetrical face
Funny eyebrows
Strange expressions
Try to love me
When I'm so wacky
You can't even
Try

Love me
When my everything hurts
When I don't have energy
To look the way
I feel
For you
And
I'm afraid to leave
The door open

Trying to love me
Is not easy
You won't get close
So fast
I may be more intense
Than you can handle
My stoney face can lie
Don't try
And love me
If you're not ready
For something
Stone precious
Smooth and rough
Tactile pleasure
My hand in yours

1. That thing I do with my face
2. That other thing I do with my face
3. Absence of facial expression
4. I am a stan for solitude
5. I will probably love my dog more than you
6. I extremely dislike most people
7. I am married to my bed
8. Tactile sensitivity
9. Emotional dysregulation sounds cooler than it looks
10. Actually, no, it doesn't sound great either
11. Have you ever heard of rejection sensitivity dysphoria
12. Come close
13. Don't leave
14. I need some space
15. I won't believe you love me
16. Anxiety brain
17. Fear of the big bad everything
18. ADHD inattentiveness
19. Weird habits
20. Rigidity
21. Fatigue
22. I'm a mess
23. An organized mess
24. Kissing
25. Saliva
26. Ew
27. I'm too clingy
28. I'm too indecisive

We've Got a Weird Dance Going On

You and I
We're rain and wind
A storm
A flood
A hurricane
A home displaced
Been torn away
In the ugly weather
We flit around like
Paper planes
There's no steadiness
We fall into puddles
Where children splash
We're too fascinating
For each other

I Am Too Tired for Companions

I pretend confidence
I understand some unnamed universes, places unseen
I wonder around wandering
Feeling too much, just enough, and nothing
I say words and wish I had never spoken
I'm a pretender of conditioned responses
I hear the silence and the hum and the chatter
I touch my arms against each other
I dream I am not floating
I see chaos
I worry and I become my worry
I try and I am circles
I want the cycling to end
I cry and there is hardly water
I hope to find the river
I am in my instinct
I am moving towards myself
I am fucking with the rules

Too Dazzling

I'm letting down
The armor around my heart
Shiny and dazzling
Why would I rid
Myself of such a thing
Fierce and strong
Too hard for swords
Too tough for you to hurt
Too tough for you to love
Maybe my heart isn't shiny
Maybe it isn't dazzling
Except for in the way
It beats
Maybe my heart isn't so fierce
So strong
Too hard for swords
Too hard for hurt
But it is
Not too hard for love

What's the Rage?

Maybe I'm more afraid
Of what's behind the anger
Like fear
Or grief
Or abounding love Maybe
I'd rather burn up
Everything that rips
This world apart
Than feel what it's like
To be out of control
Feel the unrelenting loss
Beneath my feet
Love so wildly
It feels my heart could crack
Open
Let me give you a gift
Let me show you
All that's underneath the rage

Her Red Flags

You come with her
For a little practice
Miss the target
Let the arrows fall
Try your bow again
The arrows have no points
Save those she aims at you
When no one looks
She'll watch you bleed and
Enjoy watching
She has bruises on her feet
From the dances she does
To you
Cry mercy
And she'll hold you tighter
Back away from the ones
You love

Spend your minutes on her

You'll confuse proximity
With love

You won't know
To run

Cry for mercy
She'll give you none
You'll love her all the more
You're practiced in taking arrows
You're good at learning tabletop games
But you learned too late
Even a win is a loss
With her
You have everything
And nothing
But the charm she's placed on you

Why Do I Even Care?

We were so young
It probably doesn't bother you
If it ever did
Well, it bothers me
Every time
I begin to open my heart
To the possibility
Of love
I am more terrified
Than I should have to be
Remember when you wanted me
All to yourself
Remember how you played darts
With my self-esteem
You were
The sole participant
In the game of mercy
You never gave me any Mercy
I know what love bombing is
Because of you
I know how to mason myself in
Because of you
I forget how I was
Before you
Now I am trying
To learn to love
Myself
Would that bother you

I'm So in Love with Love

I'm so in love with the idea of being new
I'm so in love with the idea of being good
I'm so in love with the idea of being wanted
I'm so in love with the idea of being held

I'm so in love with the idea of being in love
I'm so in love with the idea of being with you

I'm so in love with the idea of being I forget
I'm so in love with the act of being Too Much
         of
I'm so in love with the act of being Me

To This Time

This time, you tell me I am wonderful.
This time, you let me
tell you all my minor and major tales.
This time, you never put a hand on me
to hurt me.
This time, you teach me how to hit the target.
This time, you fall in love—
the entire freak'n package.
This time, no one begs.
This time, you are there when it's my turn
to need somebody.
This time, we dream wild.
This time, maybe we kiss.
This time, we laugh at reality—
to love would be better.

To love would be the point.

It is Enough

Our hearts have conversations
Sometimes it is enough
To hear yours beat

Dreams Cast Spells

That don't come true
Reality is cursed to come
Sometimes I want to stay in the faraway land
Where I can create my own twists
When the road seems to fork at two
Decisions
I am a Libra
Classically bad at choosing
Or maybe bad at only having wrong choices
To choose from in life
I have a little Virgo song to everything I do
It must be perfect
Or it won't do
I won't do
I am wrong
Oh
But I am also a lion
A fire
A star
I write under my own light
But I am governed by Aquarius
I carry an ocean inside me
Sometimes I will share a sip
If you stay close by
Maybe our dreams will come true

Give Me Some Time

I'm moving toward a star in the night
Trying to grasp what seems untouchable
Living more in the daylight
I'm risking flying too close to the sun
I'm risking some muscle
I let myself off the leash perfection makes
I do a little twirl
I'm working on a better twirl
One that doesn't choke on its toes
Speaking is hard
Will it always be this hard
Is using my voice a muscle
I've lost
I am terrified when it is time to show my muscle
I mostly live in silence
Only the words I write keep me company
I am working on a conversation
Give me some time

Not So Fairytale Middle

Fuck if we never see each other again
At least we shared some stories
Got some things off our hearts
Had a warm conversation
Reveled in each other's likeness
And admired where our lines didn't meet

I'm good at one times
I'm good at never agains
I'm good at making a beginning
Then running away with the middle
I'm bad at expectations

Beginnings and ends can be made
More neat
Than unkempt middles
Even when they're still chaotic
Expectations mean more
After first meetings

I am afraid of breaking a promise
I don't know how to be a disappointment
So why don't I let myself off now
Let the beginning also be an end

Fuck if we never see each other again
At least we shared some stories
Got some things off our hearts
Had a warm conversation
Reveled in each other's likeness
And admired where our lines didn't meet

But when I think of the first time
We met
Sometimes I wonder
Would the middle be worth the mess

Wishbone

I've been feeling the numbness again
You have interesting things to say
They're hard to hear over the hum of my depression
Is it the weather, the bone sucking cold
Eating at my marrow
Taking from the flavor
I want some soup to keep me warm
But nothing tastes right
Do you notice how distant I am
Do you know how close I want to be
Can you tell some of your words fly past me
I only see a shadow
I want to see the real thing
I want to hear your song
I want to rest my ears in your beauty

You Are Not Mine

I am bad at trivia
And I'm an awful guesser
I am almost always wrong
When I know nothing
Not everything is common sense
Even though I think
Some things should be
Like how calling a person
By any other name
Is not like calling a rose by
Any other name
It is not about beauty
But integrity
Though, I sometimes imagine
You as a rose
You are not mine to arrange

The Fool and the Two of Swords Could Ride the Chariot

I decide to be the fool
Leave my compass
To wander
A forest
Pretend that bears
And foxes
And wolves
Don't scare me
A bit
Let my heart lead me
Ignore the trail
Hope I find my way
Or at least
Find some joy

Maybe my heart will stumble
Upon you
The one
Who will never see me
Because they refuse to look
The one
Who always brings their arrows
To hunt
Always
Forgets
The beauty
In a dangerous thing
The one
Who always guards their heart

If they could only
Open up their heart
If I could only
Find my compass
Maybe
We could be
Unstoppable

The Holmes of Love

I conjure everything into a mystery
Something that must be turned over in my head
I am mostly a Sherlock Holmes of love
Use deductive reasoning
Before direct questions
What are the facts and the signs
What is not there that should be
In a love dance
In a fiery fancy
In a Cupid that never needed to shoot arrows
I just wait for the answer to come
Sometimes
I know I am not a great detective
And maybe romance doesn't have a meter
I'll be waiting forever if I keep making
A mystery out of every potential match

Without Question

I am more
Than everything I own
I am more
Than everything I don't have
Maybe I can open myself to the possibility
I won't get hurt
Maybe I can shoo away my guard
I've loved well before
Maybe I can love well again
Maybe I can see the victories
My heart has won
A break from battle
It's time
To stop waiting for the other shoe
To drop
It's time to experience every moment
As it comes
Realize the ability and potential for myself
To love and be loved
In all
Its gentle power
Without question

Moon Long

Are you okay, love
I haven't heard from you since
what feels a moon long

Anxious Zillennial Probs

Text, days unanswered I'll
turn it over in my
Head, where did I go wrong

But It Didn't End

I am always writing the end
Of a story
Before seeing
If it will be good

Memento, Please

I feel more at peace today
Knowing I didn't break a good thing
Before it hit the kiln
Maybe we'll also survive the firing process
Become a porcelain dish
Hold on to each other with care
So we don't crack
Or shatter from being dropped
Let's share a good meal
Or maybe many
Until this plate is just a memento
Decoration on a wall

Distance

Try at some distance
Let the red go pink—yellow
Pages, turn with care

But I Wanted You

I wanted you, but
We wanted differently
I wanted you, but
I want myself more
You don't know how
To say the hard things
The way you mean them
So you hurt me on the way
Beating around the bush

I thought maybe we could be
Friends, but
It's been a few days
And I don't think
You'll respond to my last text

If you ever do
I don't know
If I'll have space for you
Now that you've shown me
How easy it is for you to disappear

Everything is Dying, But You're So Cute

Now is the season
Where things die
But I am still growing
The chill reminds me not to be
Still so long
Sometimes I go into hibernation
Just to avoid the cold
Not knowing what to do
With the slow clock
Sometimes a frost lays over
The ground
Every crystal
Beautiful
Now it is just mud
Yesterday was rainy
I didn't want to go
Out
Even though we had plans

I'm glad
I rolled out of my grey

We sit in the car
You pet the steering wheel
As we speak
I think
You're so cute
Instead of saying this
I giggle the observation
You stop your fiddling
We dance in words

Sounds Sensual

Put my name
On your tongue
Say it gently
Like you do everything
I'll say yours
So it lasts longer
In my mouth

Wit of Aphrodite

After Sappho

I only blame

My distractions

On Aphrodite's wit

I could look

Upon you

Deep

Into the night

I Want to Tell You

When a good thing comes,
I think of you. How weird, I've
Gotten so close—fast.

Leave Your Arrows

I am undressed now,
If only these bricks would fall—
See what walls whisper
See me in my beautiful truth
And my ugly, messy life
I am vulnerable
Right now, don't bring your arrows

After They Kiss

I say her nose is glowing
She looks embarrassed
Says it's the make-up
I say I like it
She likes it too
I think I want to kiss her
But I've never kissed anyone
And my friend
She just kissed her
But she looks magical
I want some of that
Magic on me
I ask for a reading

We Won't Wait for Death

We'll create a heaven here on earth
A disco ball out of this planet
Summon water to the drought
With more than a prayer
Seed the soil to a restored Eden
Let our color light up the sky
Be the stars in the night's
Deep blue
Embrace the darkness
Its restful swaddle
Make beauty out of tattered cloths
Kiss each other's faces red
Hold on to each other through the storms
Put our heads together
Not just to think
Calm our minds on a shared pillow
Feeling each other's breath
Feeding the plants with our songs
Dancing to the sway of trees
Voguing all the way

My Little Hyena

I see your red light
Stop sign
Painting danger everywhere
Especially in failing
Falling
Where I care to stand
You are my little hyena
Always scaring away the stranger
Always more afraid
Than they know
Your spots lie
You are my pet
A feral thing
I never could control
Now I look for peace
A gentle embrace
Realize I must look
Inward
Let go
See green
A deep emerald sea
Release my hyena
Let it wander back
On the steps of real danger

No Safety Bar

Learning to love me
Is a messy line—roller
Coaster ride with no
Safety bar to hang on to
Learning to love myself on
This wild ride of life
Learning to be loved—teaching
My heart to another
Always risking being launched
From my seat—hold the divine

Smaller

Is that streak in the sky your plane
Flying up
Away from me
Standing in my boots
Looking at you leave
Staying, Staying, Staying
Staring at your vapor trail
Tapering out
As the distance between us widens
Who is getting smaller

Miss Piggy's Relationship Memes

Inspired by Margeaux Feldman

It's time to reserve my energy
Engage in relationship
With folx who are as
Invested in me as I am in them
Create space between myself
And those who would take
My time
And undo my peace

Let me be in relationships
Of mutuality and replenishment
Not of tally counting
Or pouring to depletion
Let us pour into each other
With the taste of finely aged
Joy
Let me stop settling for less than
I deserve

Let me move on from the past
Let me forgive myself for diminishing
My worth
And
Lowering my expectations

Let me give myself the love I can't
Expect from anyone
Outside this well, weathered body
Do the work of meeting myself
Every part
Especially the ones buried deep
Let me not be a puppet
Let me fall over myself failing
Find joy in the arduous climb
On this infinite journey

Not Too Cool

I want to be the cool one
Who doesn't care too much
But I know I'm the one
Who will drive things past their end
Wondering why I am so hurt
When it all crashes down
I don't know if I'll ever be the cool one
Who doesn't care too much
I love the world too terribly
I love my people to the core
I want deep consistent reciprocal loves
But I have been trained on inconsistent
chaotic lopsided relationships
I don't really want to be the cool one
I am just afraid to ask for the love I want
I am just afraid to be left again
I am trying to break old cycles
I won't let relationships happen to me anymore
I won't give up my secret heart
To a hurricane
I will wait for the love I deserve
I will be open to receiving it
I will never be the cool one
But I will care in doses that don't overwhelm

Baby Duck

I feel strung along
Like a baby duck on wheels
          You
The toddler
          Pulling me along
By a string
          Until you drop me
And run to something new
And interesting
I'm just an old scratched up
Toy
Moved by your whims
Tossed and toppled
          In your play
You don't see
          I have my own story

Stardust

If I could taste you
The scientists say it'd be
Like raspberries
In my mouth
For some reason
I think of Pop Rocks
Rock Candy
Anything firework
Anything a little
Rough stoney sweet
Anything almost
Dangerous on the tongue
Anything like a mountain tumbling
And shaking
Or a long-rugged climb
I think of me
My ruff corners
Snapping jaw
My curves
Too pronounced
My voice too sweet
I want my voice like the rocks
Like the sweet, sweet rock
Crystals of Rock Candy
And I want you
Like Pop Rocks

Why Do You Love Me?

My messy teeth
My smile that is more cringe
My face that bares it all
My chapped lips
Eczema laced skin
My anger
Always a fire
My sadness always pouring
Always a willow
Over the ponds of my eyes
Hangnails
Callused feet and palms
A little animal inside
Yelping
Howling
Growling
Trying to bring you closer
And push you away
With my puppy eyes
And owl head
I have a bark in me
Cinnamon smell
For the ants

Jumping Cars to You

One second pasted to the next
How time makes its train
We move through cars
Trying to find each other
Trying to meet at the perfect place
Not get thrown off
Jumping cars
Being reckless
Because why would I not
Reach past the enclosure to bring you in
Why would I not jump to the top
Of a moving car
When I feel so safe next to you

Change Machine

My feelings for you
Are not my feelings for anyone else
My love is not a change machine

You can't put in a dollar
And expect me to spit out quarters
My love is not pocket change
I will not clink around
Until you need me

I'll Make You Cry Laughing

My humor is charcoal dark
But I don't do cleanses
My humor is punny
That kind of funny
That sometimes elicits
A lonely kind of laughter
The best belly deep
Back of throat
Laughter
That I'll carry my lonely
Like a badge of honor
Type of laughter
That laughter that
Makes the lonely a little
Less horrifying
Type of laughter
That laughter
That's contagious
Drop dead beautiful
Rolling on the floor
Hugging your belly
Cause it's too good
Kind of laughter
That guilty kind of
Laughter
That world shattering
Earthquaking
Laughter
That says come destroyer
Take me
That wound healing
World sewing laughter
Bring me the blackest night
And I'll make you cry
Laughing

I'll make you see color
I'll make you see you
Can laugh into the pain
You can mend
Into something beautiful
Be rare and kind
Let a thing crash softly
And boisterously
In the night

Updates are Slow

You give me the links
To all the websites
Of all the people who love me
So I can see when they update
Their affections

Rag Doll

Fluff stuffed
Flat
Slumpy
Yarny-wild
All sewn
Together
All big button
Eyed
All dragged
Across
The floor
All loved
And battered
By life

But She's a Ballerina

I don't want to write about you anymore
Nickel and diming these words is too costly
I'd like to erase the moments spent
Making myself into a dummy for your sword
You know how to strike
Through the chest so well
Your strength on me was inescapable
Some people equate grace with gentleness
But you crushed me astonishing
Ballet shoes off
Behind the scenes
All I wanted to do was love you
All I wanted to do was love you
And still have me
But you demanded
I bow at your feet
Wash them with my tears
I was always never enough

Do We Want to Be Her

A woman with her sword lies in
Bed with her danger,
Chest beating like a fight song, legs ready to lift her into a
Dance
Edging her hips and toes into danger
Fighting in the light and into the night, all
Grown girl, all muscle and glimmer
Hot sweat slicks down her skin
Iron blades stay in her grip
Justice is on the tip of the sharpness she holds, she
Kindles a fire to sear her wounds closed—too many
Light only comes for the darkness, she is a
Mess of them both
Never do I remember the whole story—the entire chiaroscuro
Open to the page where she saves a village
Playing the part of so many princes before her
Quitting boy quitting girl just to be the warrior
Raising villages or saving villages—acting beside gods and men
She takes in a woman so soft
Tries to abandon her past
Unbreakable is their bond
Visiting justice upon gods and men is her redemption
Women are saved by her sword
Xena is her name
You'll find our
Zeal for her is queer, we spend our nights figuring out—do
we want to be her?

Ghost Thing

I am just a ghost
Always kissing the dawn
With my eyes open
After a sleepless night
As though my ghost thing is
Waiting for something

If the dark side of my moon is trying to
Speak to me
The whisper is too quiet
My sleep-deprived eyes are parched
No muse has come

I am just a ghost
Trying to find their headstone
But I think they forgot
To mark my grave

I am a solo artist
My ghost makes
A practice of traveling
This empty house
No one to haunt
But the body I spook everyday

I am a ghost thing
Looking
For another ghost thing
To house haunt with
So the dark keeps me
The moon is my lover
Until another ghost thing comes
To spook with me

On the Bed

No shiny love here
No rose—just crimson cape show
Only bullish act
Leave me pretending again
Pretending you are no ghost

Maybe Next Year

We eat grapes
Pretend they turn into fizzy wine
In our tummies
We are intoxicated
On New Year's Eve
Though there is no alcohol
On our tongues
We look into each other's eyes
Each reflecting the other's image
I want to kiss you
Next year

I Have Bad Ideas When I'm Around You

Death dive off a mountain after you
Eat puffer fish just because
It's what you want to do
Slow dance drunk on a rooftop
With you
It's you I want to face the deep with
It's you I want to drive
On the edge of life with
Until we fall

Looking

Looking for that sparkling lake
Looking for that smooth stone
Looking for that tall grass
Looking for the sandals
To curl my toes in
Looking to skip
Skip a stone
Turn my head
Find you
Walking
To me
Walking
In the day
Light making
A halo around
Your head, your
Beautiful face tanned
Glimmering from the rays
Do you know you have wings
Do you know we could swore

Love Bubbles

I'm blowing bubbles
Putting giddy in the air
Floating out soapy
Wobbling huge
Joy orbs
Into the blue
They are full of technicolor
Pop
It feels so good
Until it's gone

You Twist My Heart

And I don't know what this is
You twist my heart
But what should I care
I'm having the best time
Having my heart

       Origami itself about

You twist my heart
Like candy
         On the hook
I'm laughing
Because I never knew
A heart could flip like this

It's Not Halloween

I'm not a vampire
I promise
But you raise the stakes

I never said I was funny
But let's pretend to laugh

I tried to write a different story
Then you go and raise the stakes

I have phantom pains
From the hole
The last stab
Left in my heart

A Cinder

I'm giving
Little parts
Of myself
Away
Sprinkling
My affections
Like fairy dust
Making pumpkins
Into carriages
Mice into Horsies
Rags into Robes
But when the clock strikes
12
Everything turns back
Glass shatters
No one
Cheers
I'm all covered
In dust
I'm all covered
In the cleaning
And the dirt
Of the cleaning
And the stink
Covered by the sent
Of the potpourri
Mingle, Mingle, Mingle
Ugly beautiful sight
Beastly sting
Of sweet fragrance
Hurry, Hurry, Scurry
Before the music
Strikes
It's last thrum
And the wheels turn

Into vines
And the cleaning
Must be
Ran to
The dirty, dirty cleaning
That is never
Done
I thought I could be
A fairy
But I've only ever been
A cinder

Before We End

Living in a small room
With a calm dog
Is good. Talking to the dog,
Ruffling his fur
Between my fingers
Is good. Walking,
Or being walked is less good.

I do love loving my calm dog,
My dog who walks me,
Excitement swinging on his tongue
Nose deep in every aroma,
Ears twitching at each rustle.

He is really built for the chase.
He runs me towards squirrels.
I am learning to hate squirrels a little.
Just a little. I don't want to hate
Anything. I do not like people,
But I do try not to hate them.

I love living with my mostly calm dog.
Sometimes I worry about death.
Not mine. His. I experience anticipatory
Grief. I'm good at that. Anticipating
The end. I think I will grieve you every day
Before we end.

Glitter-faced Queers

We keep on meeting
We keep on connecting—we
Aren't even us—no
We are just two—two
Bodies spinning away and
Towards each other—we
Are crystal ball—glow
Glitter-faced queers—shake 8-balls
What is the future?

How Am I Doing

I'm all messed up
Rageful
And sorrowful
And loving
What is this nebula
What is this universe
Expanding
This globe slicking
Under heat
My memory
Does all
The work
Of calling you
Back to me
I wonder what
Kind of shatter
I'll hear when it breaks
When I fall
When the crowd goes
Wild
I'm just a punk
Kissing the world
In my hand
Hoping to heal
The wound
But I can't
Stitch it up
With my busted lips
I'm trying to heal
Me and the world
All at once
Let me know
How am I doing

Strange Heart

These hummingbirds make a mess of me
Their beauty flying so close in front of me
I bask in the awe of loving beings so capable
Of danger and beauty
I bask in the joy of being observed
By such beauty
Sharp
Feathery things
That chose
To show me only wonder
They have swords
In their beauty
But they've never been a danger
To my strange heart

Mx. Infinity

Drive me the long way
Just so we can catch
A few more moments
Together

Forever
Doesn't sound
So scary
When I'm beside you

We part
And it feels
Like the stretch
Of a rubber band

An expanding
Infinity
Misshapen

It could
All fall apart

Filter

I've been trucking around my trauma
Picking up the recycling
I ring the doorbell at your house
I invite you on a ride to the processing plant
The stink clings to us in the silence
When we arrive
We take all the clear
Blue and green bags
Of clinking remnants
I dump them on the moving belt
In a clunking stream
You help me sort
What will rot to poison
And what will be made
Into something new
Sometimes you ring my doorbell
I hop in your truck
It is like this between us
I don't mind the sorting
I will stay through the clinking
And clunking
And witness the remnants
And the rot

But sometimes you come around
In your pick-up truck
Painted with all the most beautiful birds
And we talk
About how we left our bags behind

He's a Traveler

I won't be revealing
My heart today
All I'll say is he's a traveler
And we met along the way
Strung together words
Until they met
In verse
And tail
I could spin you a tall story
Exaggerate the stakes
But I'm not exaggerating
When I say I like him well
A homebody
Pining after
A forever traveling Gentlebeing
I understand if you pity
My tragic love-struck heart
But I am used to suffering
I've got a leather-bound heart
Filled with ink and tree pulp
And all the things
That remind me of him
Some day he's gonna travel
And I'll never
See him again

Maybe It's Hopeless

Maybe it's not
All hopeless
Maybe we will cling
To each other
In the best of ways
Maybe we will carry
A friend
When they've been free-falling
Maybe this infinity
Of little links
Will free us
From our chains
I'm waiting
For the most unbreakable
Softness
Opening myself to all the possible
Designs
Letting myself believe
I can have a part
In making our visions
Come true
I'm scaring away
My fear of change
Welcoming uncertainty
With shaky hands
Maybe they can still
Hold a pen
Type a scene
Set a stage
Watch it all fall
Together

Ghost

I write a list
Pros and cons

Remember
How you keep
Turning invisible
The real magician
You are

I am afraid
I'm dancing
With a ghost

It's so good
It's like a movie

I try whispering
To you

And can almost
Feel your arms
Around me
As I do the dishes

In this fantasy
Your arms are made of desire
But I know you are solid
In your distance

I write letters
On stationary
Waiting for you
To reappear

How is it
I forget
You are invisible

How is it
When you arrive
The world pretends
To be a sunrise

Do you know
There are stars
In your eyes

Turning My Light Off

I think you're dimming your light for me
I think you are trying to let go, slowly
You think you can keep me
On the hook for a while
All you do is push me further
I'm turning my light off, now
I won't be an option that
You can come back to
On your time
Now it's
My turn
Now it's
My time
To tell the story
The story of the end
The flickering, fluttering end
It's ended and I'm filling my cup

Temporary Heart

You tell lies
About me
Your words slice
A knife
Through
My red heart
Whispering away
My feelings for you
In one final breath

A Toad, A Frog, A Prince

I mistook a toad for a frog
For a prince
I wanted a prince
Too bad
I put a crown on a toad
A regal frog
A royal prince
I only dream of holding you
This toad I made
Into a frog
By my imagination
A frog
Into a prince
By my desire
Desire
Makes magic
Out of imagination
Spell me something real
Let my heart stop
Cursing me
To desire

Lollipop Heart

Romantic thoughts
Of you
They're so dangerous
I count all
Your green flags
Into a bright green
Bouquet
But all I see
Is alarm red
Stop signs
On green poles
Stop lights
Emergency lights
Spinning in the dark
Flashing in the day
Showing me
Calamity
Spread out in pieces
Of heart
Like a broken
Lollipop in the road

Future Skies

The future prickles on me
Like cactus needles
Telling me to stay away
It's the sunset turning
Into a dark blue sky
Change has always been
The thing that makes
The blood run
Through my heart
The fastest
But I feel like a tortoise
Trying to skip along the way
My heart doesn't skip
When I see you
I think that's a good thing
I feel a little less like a cactus
More like a hedgehog
I'm looking into a sunset
The future is a sunrise

Love Me Like a Verb

Sometimes I want to give up
On romance

Falling in love shouldn't feel
Like walking the steps
Of a crumbling castle

Sometimes I want to give up
On blush pink passion

Sometimes I want to give up
Let my stomach acid
Take care of the flutters

Butterflies are too beautiful
To live inside me

Sometimes I want to give up
On romance
Sometimes all I want
Is for you to love me
Love me like a verb

Sometimes I want
A romance
I want the greatest romance
The butterflies
Have never seen

Will you romance me
Friend
I'll bend my achy knee
And say
Let's try
Forever
Let's try at something better
Something not falling

Subjectively Blue

I am looking for the lake
And I am looking for your eyes
I am looking for your eyes
Across the room
Holding my gaze
I am looking for the baby hyena
I am looking for your eyes
To slow my skittish heart
I am looking for your laugh
Joy is sadness' quiet
Friend
Friend
Bring joy
To my sadness
Hold my gaze across the room
Know me in a glance
Or just pretend it
I want to feel seen by you
I know
Seeing is subjective
Still, I hope we see
The same color blue

It's Not the Cookie

You aren't keeping me up
Anymore
It's just the pain
Chronic
It's just the restlessness
Endless
It's just the insomnia
Not the cookie
I'd rather be kept up
By my body
Than thinking of the
Of the way we pass
Each other
Bye
Again
And Again
When the stars
Say we should align
But what do the stars know
They just twinkle
Look at the sky
Make a wish
I'll never be yours
Anyway

Trauma Dive with an Ace

Physicality
Sex
I don't have what you're looking for
Not now
I skipped the trust fall exercise
I loved my hula hoop of space
I am fiercely in love with the inches
Between us
I am fiercely in love with desire
I am petrified of letting you in
To my hula hoop
You letting me into yours
We drop them to the ground
There is no space
Not to be physical
I am in love with the inches
That have disappeared
But sex is a messy thing
I'm not sure I'm willing
To contort myself
Into such a closeness

Wrecked for Our Friends

All the aces I know
Have crushes on their friends
We have crushes on our friends
I go to Merriam-Webster
To give me words
So I can tell you
Maybe us aces
We are more destroyed
We are more devastated
Disintegrated
Wrecked
Maybe we pack down
Push in
The ruin
For those we love
More than anyone
Maybe we know
Most people don't understand
The way we love
How the lines between
Friendship and romance
May get a bit blurrier for us
So yes, deity of words
We are more destroyed
We are more devastated
Disintegrated
And wrecked
For our friends

I Was Never Starstruck

Well maybe my heart beat
A little fast for Elliot Page
Mostly, though
I never had a celebrity
Crush
I preferred fantasizing
About emotionally unavailable
People
Who could do the job
Crush my heart
Real good
My rejection sensitivity dysphoria
Ready to bubble up

Pop

Proximity makes it all
The more possible
All the more painful

What can I say
I love walking
On hot coals
Even though
I always burn
My feet

I'm Not in Love

This is an exercise
Exercise
By taking yourself out on a date
Dress up just because you want to
Look in the mirror and call yourself handsome
Stop staring at your teeth
Draw lines over your stretch marks
With your fingers
Say "I Love You"
Mean "I Love You"
Fuck yourself
Don't feel guilty
Don't feel broken
When it feels like nothing
Say "I might be a mess, but I'm getting it together"
Say "I am worthy"
Say "It might not get better, but what if?"
Change your what ifs
Frequency over quantity
Exercise regularly
"I love you, handsome"

"Due to personal reasons, I'll be turning you into a poem"— *Melissa Broder*

Maybe if people read what is inked
You will jump out of the page
And speak
A narrative
Very different
From mine
We'll have to wait
You see
I am the magician here
I know you are used to disappearing
All on your own
Putting me on edge
A solo audience
Waiting for the other end of the magic act
The part where you dazzle me with your return
But I got tired of playing audience to the same trick
I needed to know your methods
I asked about the madness
You never tried to dazzle me like that again

Mistakes

I jumped into your story
I fucked up
Trying to get close
To a magician
This time you made flowers
Appear out of nowhere
You are always dazzling
Until it is just madness between us

Apothecary Heart

I have an apothecary heart
People keep knocking
On my chest
Trying to find a healing salve
And all they leave is poison

Romance is Weird

I'm learning love
I'm learning I could never have fallen
For you
I am learning that crushing and falling
Are dangerous things
Dangerous things we are attracted to
I looked over the ledge
I decided you weren't worth falling for
I am done falling for people
When they won't catch me
I will catch myself instead
I know I am here to catch myself
Every time I fail
At all the dangerous things
I am attracted to
I know I am here to catch myself
When the people I thought would never
Wound me so harshly
Fail
I am my own knight in shining armor
Fuck
We are all in distress
Sometimes
I know I can't save you from yourself
We can work on falling safely
It's a practice
We can catch ourselves in dance
Sometimes I don't want to take the lead
Sometimes I want a solo performance
Or to dance side by side
Wild
And
Contemporary
At your performance
Make a spot for me

In the reserved section
Our eyes will meet
The room turns silent
Still
Magnetism
Then it is all you
Until it's all me

Will you love me when . . .

You find out
I sometimes spend days
Stretched out in the bed
Not looking alive
You find out
There are days executive function
Doesn't function
Dishes pile up in the sink
The floor goes unvacuumed
You find out
I am too fatigued to smile
Or sound happy
Or enthused
You find out
Depression spools
Its silkworm body around me
Anxiety ropes around my neck
I don't believe you love me
You find out
Our communication differences
Might be a lot
You find out
What dysregulation looks like
You find out
I am restless in the night
You find out
I am always afraid

So, You Want to Romance Me?

Talk deep to me
Let's skip the inane
Fast forward
You believe in liberation
For all
Now you've got me talking
Don't shut up
About that one thing
You really love
Bring me tea
Brew it strong
Spill the tea
But only metaphorically
I'd like another cup
I'm empty
Let's go to the lady
Who reads tea leaves
And laugh at fate
Present me with a rock
But never a ring
My eyes will glow
My core will split
I will melt
Bright hot
Metamorphosis

Relationship Mechanic

I'm interested in the mechanics
Of relationships
If I could make them like machines
I would do it slowly
Turn every piece in my hand
Before placing it
Where it belongs
I'd account for any imperfections
Keep track of what needs repair
I'd take my time
Removing rust from old parts
And shining them up
Of course, none of that matters
If the pieces don't fit
If I could build a relationship
Like I could build a machine

Here is a list of parts I'd want:

1. Care
2. Curiosity
3. Creativity
4. Enthusiasm
5. Play
6. Respect
7. Stability
8. Vulnerability

Here is the rust:

1. Trauma
2. Secrets
3. All the hard stuff

The thing is not all rust comes off
We have to make up the manual
With every new machine

Go through the icky process
Of messing up
Until we are able to learn
Repair and
Maintain connections
Through times of friction

Let that tension make us turn
Hot bright dancing blue

The Plans?

I'm trying to tortoise tip
Through this thing with you
See where we go
With no expectations
Only
Slow enjoyment
Fully present in each step
Each movement
A little picture
Fuck
I'm bad at throwing out
The plans
I want a periscope
Into the future
I want to know if
This lasts

Do it Scared

Loving
Is something you must do
Terrified
What frightens you
What makes you
Jump in the night
You must face
You must court your fear
Who said
You had to fall in love with it
Put down your pruning sheers
Have you ever
Existed
Just existed
Just exist
Maybe your fear is a hound
Let her sniff your hand
Maybe your fear is a snake
Watch him slither
You don't have to touch
The scales of your fear
You only have to
Exist with it
Exist with it so
It can never become
Your king
Exist with it
In loving
What
You
Must

Horror Isn't Romance

I'm just looking for a human
Who will stand beside me
Sit across the room as I
Write a love poem about them
First, I should probably quit
Fantasizing about the perfect poem
To write my Cinder? Cinderella? love into
Yearning is a weird word
It is uncomfortable to say
Yearn-ing
Doesn't give you butterflies
Yearning gives you a poisoned apple
A choking ribbon
A good old horror story surprise
Remember when her head fell off
And the last gasp of breath left you
Do you really want to see the violence
Behind wanting
I am over yearning
I am done with taking my heart
On roller coaster rides
I'm looking for a human
I can love myself beside
I am looking for discomfort
That closes gaps
I am looking to take my heart away
From the amusement park
I am looking for the calm
Not a storybook life

For the First Time

Trust in yourself
Let the wild
And trained
Sides of you
Meet
Match each other's stride
Don't let go
Do shake your mane
Don't let anyone
Make you
The fool
Again
Don't crack your skull
Jumping in head-first
Stop denying
Yourself
Let the world spin
Slow
Beneath your feet
Don't ignore
The rumble
The bark
The squirrel chitter
And the bird song
For once
Sing
Like it's your first
Song
Let yourself break
Into a smile
When the crowd stands
In applause
When you meet them
Outside
The doors

Give them a second
Look
Maybe
You didn't see them
Fully
The first time

Acknowledgments

First and foremost, thank you to my wonderful editor Elle Warren, whom without my book would be a mess only understandable to me. I would also like to thank my amazing photographer, Sadie Randall. She made me feel comfortable in front of the camera and is responsible for contributing to a gorgeous cover. I can not forget to thank Joy Sullivan's Sustenance Writing Community for giving me the courage to move forward with this project. I love the folks in my core group. Thanks to my friends for encouraging me, and being my loves. Thank you to every person who has showed me what love is, and taught me what love is not.